THE GLISTENING SOUL

THE GLISTENING SOUL

Sweta Parmar 'Nicky'

DIVE IN THE OCEAN OF KNOWLEDGE
Ocean Books

Ocean Books Pvt. Ltd.

ISO 9001:2008 Publishers

Published by
Ocean Books (P) Ltd.
4/19 Asaf Ali Road,
New Delhi-110 002 (India)
e-mail: info@oceanbooks.in

ISBN 978-81-8430-521-0
The Glistening Soul
by Sweta Parmar 'Nicky'

Edition
First, 2017

Price
₹ 200.00 (Rupees Two Hundred only)

Printed at
R-Tech Offset Printers, Delhi

Dedicated to my
Respected Parents
And my baby Shreejita
Maa-Papa
I always need your lovely blessings

Dedicated to everyone who wonders if I am writing but I am writing because we all exist. It is for all those who walk and read at the same time as I do. To all those wonderful people, who inspired me to write.

The journey of life
Is full of
Pits 'n' Pitches.
Many obstacles
But if one is sure
On top, one'll surely
.....Reach(es).

ACKNOWLEDGEMENTS

Always when I sit down to write, seems that the creation which is done by the carving of words as a joyful yet solitary one. Just like it's only my soul and me. Then, gradually, the circle begins to widen, analysing more and more people, all of whom contribute their expertise, until you are holding this carved creation in your hands. Some people acquired a very special place and part of the ever widening circle of this creation that allowed me "The Glistening Soul" to reach you all.

Thanks a ton to my little Angel, Yoshima, who worked emotionallyside by side encouraging my potential. Along with her father, Sanjay, who contributed his critic knowledge and probing questions to help me unite the words which has made me a better writer. Thanks to my brother, Vikrant who always has hidden faith in my calibre. Thanks to young lad Ayush who always listen's to my penning patiently and helped in improving.Thanks to my vision and thinking which captured sight through the inner graphics and thanks to ,Ishita Bansal, who created front and back cover. Thanks to all those who helped me in the layout and to give a new look to the beautiful world of readers.

Heartiest courtesyto my parents and in laws for their spiritual guidance, love and wisdom. Thanks to my friends and family for their unstinted and continued support and appreciation for my work. And with deepest gratitude to those close ones who are not with me now but have helped me to discover the truths of life and who left their marks on my mind through which I, along with you all, might discover the reality at the right time - that indefinable life-changing moment when we have the inner eyes to see and the soulful ears to hear.

Thank you, Thank you, Thank you to you all.

With heartiest Regards, Presenting this poetry bouquet to you all.

—Sweta Parmar

MY TAKE

This creation is a collection of poetic reflections that is intended not only to inspire but motivate you to lead a renewed life. I tried that each one of these poems can derive a different perspective or reflection in your life. I have been penning down feelings for few years whenever I found and felt something interesting.

"The Glistening Soul", is a collection of same feelings. The ideas and reflections in this creation are penned by my own words and verse though it may relate to any other verse in some view-points.

I think let us all live our lives by full Confidence, Positivity, Faith and Hope. We should try to adjust our attitude for the better life, making others smile too. Here is my collection...

Read.......
Reflect.....
Renew .....

CONTENTS

1

THE WAY OF LIFE

The way of life is very complicated,
sometimes very formal and sometimes exaggerated.
Wandering in the dreams in snow on sleigh,
none is having a little time to lay.
Always roaming on a roller coaster ride,
no matter what though afraid of slide.
Earlier the feelings are from heart,
which always remains the same as in start.
Time is the best healer as well as the killer of emotions,
nothing to be changed when divided into fractions.
Seldom the mode turned around and played as a game,
never again the real life remained the same.
So much anger is wrapped around in heart,
without any solution of tearing apart.
Moreover some say...... love you like life,
sarcastically they are amazed to make someone... A wife.
The way to travel is full of pits 'n' pitch(es),
so many obstacles but if one is sure ....reach(es).
Nevertheless the destined "will" is made to mature,
looking at the sky and ready to assure.

May be in doubt if its not a dream,
Oh! the way of life should be covered without a need of scream.
So many wishes come along with the deeds,
with all the zeal it meant to succeed.
The way of life one passes swinging, swirling,
getting all the assets swaying in the mood of singing.
Completing the journey as a successful individual,
a daughter, a wife, a mother and an author as gradual.
Everyone has there way of life to survive,
and zest with enthusiasm to fight to strive.
Always ecstatic to move with awesomely wonderful smile alive,
getting gracious or gorgeous and walk through .... the way of life.

□

2

THE WHEEL OF TIME!

The wheel of time is revolving
non-stop,
motion with emotions are repeating
atop.
Fortune creates the journey as
smooth,
destined perfectly no reason as being
truth.
Flowing as Mandarin in different stream throughout,
breaking cages and flourish through
breakout.
Brightened with the lightening sky
ahead,
scratching at the edge with the bang of
head.
Nevertheless the rotating clones of
shades,
wearing the gloves with holding
spades.
piercing beneath the blissful
memories,

peeping under the dreams of
journeys.
Sickening as for emotion are so less
now,
saddening not for so much care
somehow.
Useless things kept running across
mind,
screaming always kept running ...
Abind.

□

3

JOURNEY WITHIN!

Wandered whole night unspecified, unidentified
Forgetting the stream unknown, unsaid
Making all efforts to summarise or recall
But journey within is not so easy at all

Several incidents unfolds 'n' folded again
rhyming about happiness in memories regain
sometimes hypertensed sadness to avoid
breaking through the world of silence so wide

Too many words running in the mind
they seemed to be together and kind
playing with the emotions and trying to be a finder
they don't sing always in joy and hinder

Always keep power to get visions of dark night
dreamed of joy departed but an awakening dream of
life and light
living in the dark with the candle in heart
writing an unwritten poem with emotions apart

Hearing from mind the.... unspoken words inside
understanding the meaning of... feelings beside
slept dreaming the ways of existence
waking up thinking deeds of excellence

Living whole life, knowing ...whoever loves you like life
surviving with fact that, why ...you are alive
Have been writing but ....seemed... lost the words
but however have some to...cost the swords

It seems ....dying ...without finishing the poem
as all the emotions cant be penned down in a slogan
the journey within will last one day
vanishing with the soul n be lost someday.........

□

4

EVERY-TIME

I am gazing with the twinkle in mah eyes
and .. EVERY-TIME
I see myself in your adorable smiles
just a look...... at you
and you always seemed to be created perfect
nevertheless.....or more
but a masterpiece with all the special effect
whether ....it's
dark at night ,or, in shining daylight
your....aura
as always have a spark of miraculous light
it's...... awesome
when you look at me even for an instance
my .....heart
skips a beat and wants to vanish the distance
when....ever
you speak anything or just mumble
I....feel
there is something in mah stomach that grumble
not.....only
you but your imagination makes a chill run down
spine

The Glistening Soul

no.......doubt
you are Almighty's perfect creation as the best
and......forever
i want you to be mine and want to keep my head
on.....your
shoulder and close my eyes for the last time whenever
I rest
EVERY-TIME...... forever till I am dead.

□

5

THE FRESHNESS

Early morning when I wake up fresh
come out of room and have no stress
with so many positive feelings to express
and I know it'll all be hidden and suppress

Life is a wonderful journey to travel
many struggles and hives to Ravel
but if we never lose hope n strangle
very soon we'll be out of trouble

So I keep the zest to move forward
and ready to face every trouble though; awkward
but when we kick out from our mind that coward
none can beat the zeal inside us to move forward

Life is awesome to live to the fullest
and filling every moment with happiness
no matter what happens in future
but there are so many dreams to nurture

I am doubting my creation
as I am lost in a desolation

I just want to run free
not losing the faith in thee came to know and reach
conclusion

Thought, desolation is the only consolation
now there is nothing to fear with emotion
as I spend the final moments in desolation
But, I should not live in isolation
And carry rest of journey with sensible clarification

6

STRUGGLE

A bee in the hive
want to take a dive
outside it wants to see
the world so beautifully derive
but not so wonderful always it is
sometimes a bit tough it seems
not every road is smooth to walk along
there are many ups n down to feel among
so many tests to clear of life
not every single is easy to survive
struggle, struggle 'n' struggle all side
to keep oneself to live abide
what is the solution of living a life
is there a way one has to survive
no obstacles or stops to hide
and walking along a way to decide

7

HIDDEN TREASURES

So many challenges we have to face,
just to take everything to surface.
As things are getting underneath to pace,
when we didn't get anything for space.

Not always we have to rear,
keeping in the mind why we have the fear.
If I have my life in my hands with steer,
then I'll drive it with my hands holding gear.

If we keep ourselves with the spirits so high,
and if we never think negative and never sigh.
Always will we get the wings of success to fly,
and keeping the happiness besides too to imply.

Seldom we think if we have the limits,
but never we think why we always commit!
for feelings which we seldom submit,
is very rare to make a summit.

Balancing the things with mind and soul,
taking the opportunity and setting a goal,

walking along avoiding the pole,
as to live the life to the perfect and whole.

We have to be confidante keeping fears aside,
and believe in the life keeping faith inside.
For so many talents and values we hide,
and now these hidden treasures should be shown worldwide.

□

8

CHANGE

In mah life , there are lot of things
To get them changed I always wish.
Words in the moments ..always stay
That I wish....... I didn't say.

Sometimes all I can think of Is you.
when I open my eyes for shadow I knew
I live for the sunlight But everything is grey.
But most times all that I think of, is far away.

Though I've tried But nothings changed.
I tried and I've tried But the same it stayed.
I gave everything To save what's in you.
I gave everything as want to change nothing in y

Now I feel you in me like my beating heart.
I sit on the beach and I look at the stars.
And I realise all we are, is waves on the sand.
which comes 'n' goes with every upcoming stra

9

THOUGHTS

Through my head
..millions of thoughts run
Thoughts of remorse and things I have done
memories of happiness along with saddest thought
Times of friendships from the thoughts of past
But now I have some beautiful thoughts to memorize
Thoughts of family and those who are close to me
to reprise
But then…
I think of my daughter whom I'm proud
by being blessed
Every day with ... And .. for the achievements she
accomplished
I think of my hubby
Who's the love of my life
And the one that I failed the most.
Being the part of his life
day-to-day
.. I wonder.. how I go..
With so much on my mind and scarcely time to row....
I want to apologize to the ones I love,

And how I failed the good Lord above.
I feel .. I have lived in sin,
Haunted by memories.... of what I did.....
within
This is my punishment, I have to accept,
Being tormented in my mind by things
to disconnect
I want to forget everything but not only to be paused
For all the hurt and suffering that I caused
To the adultery and lie's I told to break the bound
There is no way to turn this around,
But I learn from my actions and prey for forgiveness...
and want to spend a life full of happiness
wandering in my memories with the thoughts of present
trying to build my future to get everywhere to represent
thoughts, thoughts, and thoughts in mind
always coming back 'n' forth to rewind.

□

10

NOT ALWAYS

Not always the world is beautiful
Not always the mind is zestful
Not always the mood is cheerful
Not always the gesture is graceful
Not always the persona is tactful

Though the world is full of beauty and nature
With all the things to cherish n nurture
But not always we wander as a traveller
As life is not only a plan as philosopher
Sometimes we need to go to an astrologer
Do we really want to know what is in future

How can it be possible to believe in it by paper
Oh! Is the God now came within us as predictor?
Being a human we have to think very clear
Do we have to believe or not in fake readers
This is not only state of mind of achievers
Just giving few important things as an advisor

Not always the life is beautiful
Not always the mind is zestful

□

11

BARREN LAND

Barren is the land of Kutch,
having so many wrinkles as such!
No water since the land is dry,
let the people strive 'n' cry.

Sand is turned into pebbles then stones,
as hard as it is hard to re tone.
Thirsty eyes quenching to get wet,
hoping the clouds shower to melt.

Same is the lives of human beings now,
want so much and don't want to stow,
think as life is bundle of opportunities,
but don't bother to run and catch them in mitts.

Whenever a stone comes on way while walking,
none bothers to keep it aside and forwarding,
some jump and some walk from a side,
and that small stone never get ..... aside.

If we have a little courage to hold,
that small stone in our hand ...behold,

we can make a building collecting it together,
as we put the pebbles in the water to fuller.

Just think.....if we put a little labour on aim,
Surely.....we get our all destinational fame!

☐

12

RAINDROPS

The sound of sprinkling which
I hear at night
I thought may be my tap is trickling
and not closed tight

But when that sound merged
Into a showering tone
The ears are alert
and gazed towards the phone
As an individual residing alone
getting scared and moved to be known

Towards the window to peep through a hole
may be its only an illusion to be told
Rhythmically crawling towards the shade
listening own heartbeat with speed

As soon as the curtain is removed
the sound seems loud and legs didn't move
But gathering whole courage
behaving as a grown
the sight of outside assumed to frown

Giggling were the sound of laughter
as if there was no monster
enjoying the music of the sound ...
that is created
by the RAINDROPS falling on the road and floated

Showering the water and wetting everything
the best season of life comes in many things
just grab the drops into your fist or palm
and dance in the rain with full ecstasy and charm

Never will one get the opportunity so bright
dancing in the rain with the rainbow colours in sight

□

13
IDENTITY

Sometimes we lost our identity
and find too sometimes
but sometimes it is at the loss of dignity
though we get it back sometimes

As the time moves on
and the mind swings
the memories of love 'n' trustful moments
comes within to bring smiles
but suddenly it turns to tears
when the memories of blame 'n' hate
comes on way with smears

Those were the days when a glowing charm
always fascinates the gracious
and were the days when only emptied eyes
were gazing with a hope of being precious

The words of appreciation....
were a part of life
which changed into curse ...
and always cut as knife

Pinning inner soul and making to bleed inside
Though not visible but scared and unable to subside
They say that as time passes bad memories fades
But with the time it's remember with different shades.

□

14

YOU.........ME

You............ Are All This To Me!

My hopes...My dreams...
My cries...My screams...
You're all this to me!

My now...My then...
My beginnings...My end...
You're all this to me!

My laughter...My tears...
My shrieks...My fears...
You're all this to me!

My life...My death...
My silence...My breathe...
You're all this to me!

And with all my love
this is where you'll always be...

My truth.. My lies...
My confession... My secret...
you're all this to me!

My inside... My outside...
My soul... My shadow...
you're all this to me!

You trust...or... don't...
You believe... or..not...
I am alive… means …
you are in me!

□

15

LIFE

Life comes and goes
so lets live it fully.
life is too short
to keep fighting and downgrading.

As we all grow old in this wildly life
we realise what this world has come to us alive

life comes and goes
so live it up all
you never know when you'll take in that air to finish
it all.

Life comes and goes
so lets have a party from night...
till morning from evening to night

so party hard
because tomorrow is never promised
some people take it for granted
before they demised

Some people aren't here
some people are here
from tough times we may have less power
but suicide isn't the answer

Life is hard we all know it to be
so lets take time out of our day
to pray best for another day

So remember this always
Life comes and goes
Let's live it fully
Let's live it all

□

16
COUPLET

Every couplet of mine is just for you
Oh! My soulmate ...and...
All my poems belong to you

My confession of love for you
.. are my poems
be it my mind, my heart or my soul

My thoughts are moulded in the frame of words
My emotions are elicited.... again.... into words
My feelings are poured on the pages
with emotions
I am not any poetess
... I swear ..but a creation

I have found my "twin flame"
in you
My only frame is to be absorbed in you
Oh!"my twin flame", come and hide me holding tight
Avoiding this world ...take me far away from every
ritual and rite

I may feel what is meant to be ...the "me" in "myself"
I perceive "the real me" as.... being .."the higher self"
It is an "ecstasy" for me......to love you
My life's every moment is phoenix with you

Oh! My "twin flame love"
"My completeness"
Is discovered by you
The one who made me gain my "wholeness"
Is you

Every vicious and every gentle in me is all your belongings
In my life..You are the reason behind all my hopes and happenings

I swear
......My every couplet is just for you
All my poems and phrses belong to you
and only .... you!!!

□

17

STRONG

I wanna make this clear
I want you with no fear
I don't want to be friends
Or just someone
You depend on all the time

I want to be that Strong Woman in your life
that holds you tight
You know the one girl you can't stop thinking
or talking about
I know.....is me

For us to have that one song
I just want you to realise with me
is where you belong
You came into my life so unexpected
Neither looking for love just stuck in reality

We found comfort in each other
A connection like no other
Whether we are lovers or the best of friends
I'm by your side always to the end

I love our honesty, stubbornness
Being hundred with each other
We may shout and fight
But that ain't nothing cause
We been together so long

I don't ever want to change you or hurt you
Or make you something you're not
But for you my life I can do a lot
As you have seen
I want to take you to places
You have never been

All I ask is respect, love, loyalty
I will do the same for you
I trust you with my soul, heart, my life
I m a strong woman
But shouldn't have you to b scared

'Cause I know how much you truly care
We live or Die are Best Friends,
Lovers n soul-mates
Forever'

□

18

LOVE....LIGHT

Love brings a light
That always shines
No matter where you go
It warms the heart with energy
And these a special glow

Love reaches out with gentleness
And make your dreams come true
Love takes the precious things in life
And brings them all to you.
I'll never stop loving you my life

It's true
I'll always be caring
The way that I do
I'll always be needing
The warmth of your smile
To brighten my world
And to make it worthwhile

I'll never stop loving you,
Dear Life... I Vow

You'll always mean just
What you mean to me now

Whatever the season
The day or the year
I'll never stop loving
And needing you Dear!!!

□

19

YOU MAKE ME

I've never felt this way before
I've never been confused
Strong and yet so sore
I believe it's what we call love
I've never thought
It was innocent as a dove

You make me want to act tough
You make me do all those crazy stuff
You set my soul free
You make me fall to my knee

You make me act all strange
You make me want to change
You make me smile
You make me show my romantic side

You're the one and nothing is above you
You're the best and I love you
Your name is written above my heart
And nothing can tear our love apart

□

20

I DECIDED

I admit the truth and reality.
As
I don't want to lose him as he is my life
I hate my ownself when my soul wants to befool me .
I hate that I didn't have that impact and trust what I had once on him
I decided to choose silence being solitary
I admit the truth of not in his family
I hate when he do formality being scared for a minute
I hate that he is unable and deny to accept his priorities
I decided to choose silence being solitary
I admit the truth and reality
I accept him with his all bad and good, truth and lie
I hate myself when same things he won't accept and deny
I want him to love me truly without compromising
I want him to be true to himself
I love him beyond limits and so do he I think
Then
Why I am still living solitary

And he is not allowed to come in my dreams
I don't want to lose him as He is my life
For this
I decided to choose silence being solitary
I admit the truth and reality

□

21

DIFFERENT

Two strangers side by side,
Walking along the same route.
The route is same though,
But they are alone at every row.

Different people on different side,
On same route to walk…they decide.
Think the destiny is better or worst,
May be they're just scratching the crust,
Different is the persona of what they thrust.

As a fact that opposites attract,
Their different ways came on track.
Following the same route and way,
Getting along hand-in-hand they sway.

Smiling curves making them radiant,
For they have now destination…through pavement.
No more are they lonely now,
As they have power of two….. Somehow.

One day they will shine as stars,
Being besides each other with attires.

□

22

TOO HARD

It's so hard to sit beside your bed
And waiting for a thought to come
As with no reason it seams to shed
A tear which is waiting outcome

It's too hard to wait for someone
And harder to ignore that someone
It's hard to listen that I will change
And harder to believe again 'n' again

It's hard to see that someone crying
And harder to stop self-rather denying
It's hard to see that someone to suffer
And harder to go back again 'n' whisper

It's hard to wait for getting things to be fine
And harder to believe it and scare with crime
It's hard to see someone wants you more then life
And harder to trust again and give up on …rest of …
LIFE

It's hard, it's hard and it's really hard to survive
But it's harder and even hardest to strive

□

23

DREAMING TRUE

Listening to the rhyming drops
Mind is wandering at the top
Wishing Oh! You come here and stop
Ask me for a cup of coffee and started talking non-stop

Constantly gazing at you
When you hold my hand with fingers locked
My heart started beating loud
Like a clock is ticking Tic-Tok

It is an act for a minute
But passed as in fraction of seconds
A moment captured
When you hold me tight
Can be cherished for the lifetime insight

Then suddenly feeling of the loosened grip
Picking up the glass from the table to sip
Taking a long breathe and controlling the beat
Running towards another end to prepare the treat

Sounds of laughter feels like enchantment
Just bring coffee without any resentment
Dreaming the sequence wearing soft satin nighty
Didn't know it'll come true and blessed by The Almighty

Sparkle in the eyes thinking
As I were sitting in the desert
A hand came close and hold me tight
To get me, though exert

Making me to believe
That I should not fear
Whenever I need I'll get that hand
Whether far or near

Now realised why people hold hands
It's not just to say that it's till the end

It's a hidden, unspoken message
Behind the touch
No matter what but I'll always love you
So much
Too much of care sometimes cause trouble
So, hold the hand tightly
And move with a mumble

Ah! It's a true dream ...
I realised
As soon as the heat ...
is applied
Oh, Jesus! I burnt my hand
And my real dream is still sitting
At the other end....!

□

24

GLISTENING SOUL

Looking at the sky
Comparing who is more empty
Whose love is bigger
And whose's scanty

When someday life'll leave
And you have no option
Then to believe
That who's the one
Whose love'll be huge

The one who is still with life
Or the one who's gone

Darkness is not so bad
Your eyes'll adjust being sad
But the one who's gone is more lonely
And has huge loss as they say
For the one who has life has got
So many people to pray

With life one can talk, walk, see and feel
But they couldn't have a single moment to heal
At least you've that option, that only you got their soul and see them inside
But they've to bear the pain of sharing you with everyone beside

They say "I am alone", but they are not
People'll say "May they rest in peace"
But they wouldn't
The one with life have so many people
Who can give them comfort
While sharing and they'll feel it too

But the one who's gone
Is all alone up there
With the memories of having you
Only within the soul
And finds comfort only with you

□

25

YOU IN ME

With my emotions I feel you
as my eyes cannot see
With the vibrations I hear you
as my ears cannot hear

So,
In-between you and me
I am the one counting extras on you
as I cannot be
The best I can reveal is
what I feel is beautiful

If you can feel comfortable in explaining me about
what I'm missing
I can't explain how much I'll love hearing that from
You
You say someday we'll be together
Is that an appeal?

If it is then you can believe
that I can smell the senses you hear
But one thing seldom I fear!.....
If we're on wrong page

You know people would've laughed
If they knew that we would fall for one another
As they thought
we doesn't equal anyway
But, I'm sure with time
they'll realise as with time
and patience we made things to workout finely

And I just hope what you want with me
is not a part time thing
Because what I want is you in me
It's not that I'm looking to be stress-free
The things wouldn't be same by the passing time
With the heart, formal feelings can be exchanged

The values can be decreased with limited talks.
May be the days could be limitized into hours and minutes
May be the trust could replace
and we're not the same

But, just remember one thing
that in the end,
There'll be only you in me
and me in you
Our soul will always be the same
without change
And we'll be the same "US"

26

MAGICK

Your presence so near I always feel
I want you to hear
wiping all your deep 'n' dark fear.
On my face I sat your gaze
where my love's embraced
All those fallen tears we can forget.
Your sweet smile with tender care I feel
Your sense is so deep and warm
Always giving me a glowing charm
My whole life turned around at your laughs
Whenever I feel your passion and talks
I want to feel the ecstasy when we meet after long
And, all those enchantments of your spell
Feeling deep inside with every beat
So, is, our secret destinies....
fulfilling our lives
The dream of us fills our soul with bliss
Our eternities will sparkle for a love so true
The sun will be shining
with sweet pictures of me with you

□

27

FEEL

Watching my own shadow
Sometimes I feel
How it always be different
At every point on turning heel

When I move
Sometimes it becomes so long that seems Height won't last
And sometimes it's so short that seems
we're playing hide 'n' seek

Creating different pictures from fingers in hand
Sometimes dancing moves 'n' sometimes a bird to bend

It feels to be happy by watching own creation
Though with the shadow it comes up with the imagination

A bird or an animal, a flower or a kart
Whatever is made but comes out from heart

To feel the passion 'n' love behind every shadow
A pure heart is needed to carry it on beyond the shadow

□

28
EMOTIONS

Walking through the street
Just want to get retreat
Sitting on the couch bed
Thinking many a things if
Blues are shed

What it feels with the grievance
Pain
When heart is aching but all in
Vein
How could one be so merrily happy
When so many stress is there in its
Lap...py

Strange feeling of stunned experience
Hard to believe but yet at preference
Traces of anger when heart beholds
Mind is strained and it shouldn't be hold
Ecstatic were the memories
Which bring smile at liveries

Saying to remain being quite
And look what's there insight
Ohhhh! What a fun it is to walk
Through the memory lane
And travel once again with different
Emotions but not so plain

□

29

WHERE

Whenever I feel lost
I don't wanna found
Always I think
Where do I go ?
When I look and want that peace in my heart
But I know that I'll never hear that sound
Always I think
Where do I go?
Whenever I wanna cry but I try to laugh
I try to keep living as I'm not ready to die
Always I think
Where do I go?
Because the sun never seems to shine now
Whenever I ask
Can you give back mah life
Its mine and not yours
Don't know now
How to keep going
How do I fight this
Always at that time I think
Where do I go?

As now I'm tired of feeling beat down
Still I'm trying with all my might
Don't get the answer
Where do I go
When my head hang too low
Please someone give me reply
As I just don't know
And Always I think
Where do I go?
I asked again
Does it take tooooooo long?
If I find that peace and place where I belong
Ohhhh! my heart 'n' soul
I need you to help me
And take a valid stand
I'm so scared to do it myself
Please will you hold my hand?
As usual I'm in a dilemma
Where do I go?
Where do I go?
Where do I go?
Do you know?

□

30

SMILES

She smiles
Her eyes sparkle
She laughs
She is full of energy
She moves
The wind starts singing
She turn her head around
The shine is glistening

But…… inside

She is hollow
Behind her sparkling eyes
Are held back tears
Inside her laughs
Are hidden cries
She stands tall
With weights in her hand
Within Every line
Is a hidden lie

But ....

Not every time
The laugh is artificial
Not every time
The glitter is fake
Not every time
The weight seems heavy
Not every time
The truth is a lie

Sometimes.......

She smiles
With glittering eyes
She laughs
Truly full of energy
As the dream she dreamt
Are now about to accomplish

□

31
DAUGHTER

My dear sunshine
My dear daughter

You're so wonderful
You're my pride

You're my joy
You're my pleasure

Through good times
And in strife

I love when you chip in when
There's work to be done

I love your cute laugh when
You're just having fun

Are you smarter or prettier?!?
I can never decide

I love everything about you
My sweet little Angel
And that's what I say

Be my soul-mate daughter
In every birth 'n' day

You're a special person
Till I'm alive 'n' after too

I say I love you more
In every way 'n' what you do!

□

32

FRIEND

I think of you
And all the days we've spent
And the days
We'll be spending together

You are my bestfriend
You're my soulmate
And I know
You'll always be there until the end

Your shoulder to cry on
Will always be there
Whenever there is something wrong
And whenever time is tough
You're always there

The way you do things
Show me your love and care
Though we are separate in ways
You'll always remain in my heart

None in this world can see
How special you're to me
You're my strength
You're my power
My bestfriend, my soulmate

I always dreamed of
A friend like you
And when I found you
It was like dream come true

You understand the worst side of me
That none can ever see
You're the best person I've known
My bestfriend, my soulmate

Together…It is always that
We smile and we cry
We keep our every secret
And will cover our each sorrow

As we are best of friends
Till the day we die
We'll always be with each other
Whether living or after we die

The friend like you is hard to find
You came in life when none cared
We've been through good 'n' bad times
And everything we shared

And now we'll made us laugh
When we are sad
As now you are the only one

My bestfriend, my soulmate
I feel that you are
Like a ray of sunshine
Always present with me
Whenever the world is dark

You will guide me through bad times
I believe
And will wipe away my tears
I can see
As now you are only
My bestfriend, my soulmate

We're like two bodies and a soul
You're the best amongst the best
Though our time together
Is passing day by day
But........now
Until the very end
You'll always be my bestfriend

My bestfriend, My soulmate

□

33

DARE

When a new day begins,
Dare to smile gratefully
When there is darkness
Dare to shine glistefully

When there's injustice
Dare to condemn as first
When there's something wrong
Dare to do it anyway

When life seems to beat you down
Dare to fight back amazingly awesome
When there seems no hope
Dare to find out some

When you're feeling tired
Dare to keep going
When times are tough
Dare to be tougher

When love hurts you
Dare to love again

When someone is hurting more
Dare to help in heal

When something is lost
Dare to find it anyways
When a friend falls
Dare to extend your hand

When you cross paths with another
Dare to make them smile
When you feel great
Dare to help 'n'create

When the day has ended
Dare to feel as you've done the best
When you wanna feel great
Always dare to be at the best you can
At all times my dear friends
Dare.............. to live with smiles!

□

34

RELATIONSHIPS

Whenever
Times have been tough
And things have gone wrong

The deep love we share has been there all along
there's nothing that's right
And you say why to go on?
we continue to fight
But we never give up

A light of love was there
that gives us our sight
we know there is light
Though our hearts may get dark at times
Situations between us were not fair
But inside we get through it
As of something special we share

You were aware of the way we feel
Through the trials we make
A love that is so very real

And not so fake
At times it seems like a raw deal
We must get through these trails
Until we are healed

You feel there's no hope
As trials are not easy
you feel you're at the end of your rope
And started feeling dizzy
You must go down deep in the pit of your heart
Get to stop your despair and give a new start

True love for each other is a rare gift some get
when that trial comes, don't ever forget
To remember that
there is a rare thing we share that had to come from above
And those trials will end, what you got through was pure love

□

35
DARKNESS

Winds were blowing hard
And walking through the jungle
Scared to the depth of heart
But no one was there to mingle

Oh! So dark is the day
And it's not even the night
Woods are so deep
It's hard to breathe tight

But we've to walk along
Across the terrifying beauty
Daring to move without belong
To courteous or encouraged duty

As the lovely dark forest wandered
I m nowhere but still pondered
Do I have a place now to survive
And got the answer that I've to strive

Oh! High kings covered with leaves
Let us escape as we're not thieves

Little kids awaiting there
They'll be scared as I get late rare

Lemme reach to my destination 'n' home to take care
of my elders 'n' all to whom I belong
Tough is this journey in the woods within
Rough is the way to reach out and begin

Remembering those words by Robert Frost
I always rhyme whenever feel defrost
That the woods are lovely, dark 'n' deep
I have several promises to keep
And miles to go before I sleep

And.... Miles to go
Before..... I sleep!!!!

□

36

STARS

Sitting on the terrace
Watching up above the horizon
Thinking to stare at the stars
And have a glance to their wars

In-between the moon is glittering
So big, round and bright
Thinking to talk to the moon
Is not only dream but a boon

Sky is covered with the Stars twinkling
Which one to count so many are blinking
Sometimes it feels thar stars are falling
Down towards us they are beaming

Like I am on the ground
And stars are scattered
On a summer night
And we are flattered

I've heard some stars may fall
And I'm here to catch them all
But seldom is that lucky night
When I catch them with my fist so tight

Then again I look above
I can see some stars of love
Feeling as if they are coming near
I am feeling and start to move

Some stars are good
Some are too kind
Some are only yours
And some are mine

Just wanted to tell to the stars
To shine for me too bright
And Lemme keep them in mah eyes
After seeing the best glance tonight

□

37

DADDY

Oh Daddy!
I love you so
But why
I am always misunderstood
Why always I have to wear hood

Oh Daddy!
I am your little girl
And I love you so!

Sometimes I try not to hear
But can't help not to hear
When you tell me what to do
I am always listening to you
I always think I am your little baby
And I am thinking this just may be

I always hide my unsaid depression
As I want to make good impression
Because I wanna show to this world
That I am also a better than best girl

I sometimes let go all the worries
Because I am still not that Daddy's little angel
So here I stand so confidante
And want each 'n' everyone to understand
That I also want time and space which I need
No need to worry that every time I have to plead

I know I am Daddy's little misunderstood
And I would never Lemme go so easily
So that none wanna leave me alone
And I can be me whom everyone should be known

□

38

PROMISES

Some says that many a times though spoken
That promises are always meant to be broken
But as it is in human nature captured throughout
That not every promise is broken and can workout

Though the pattern never changes
It always remains the same
And we always use that excuse
May be with different name

So many reasons we have to give
To decide and let others to forgive
Thinking may be next time it will be true
The promise which you keep a due

Promise to keep happy
Promise to keep calm
Promise to keep patience
Promise to keep alarmed

Promise to give the best
Promise to be positive

Promise to be joyous
Promise to get victory

Promise to take care
Promise to never forget
Promise to keep clean mind
Promise to forgive all

Promise to never hate anyone
Promise to be kind to all
Promise to always be true
For every other relation
Who possess you

So many promises with your little heart
Will keep you always to get a new start
And it'll never let you feel down
At any moment you don't have to be sad 'n' frown

Promise yourself one thing
Never to hurt whom we care
Promise yourself on more things no
To be sunshine in others lives

Because..... for some
Promise means everything
And once it's broken
Then....
Sorry means nothing!!!!

□

39

LOST LIFE

The snow is glistening
The wind is whistling
We try a lot to avoid
But we're all listening

Very loud are the screams
Very bad are the dreams
Though it is so very far
But so close it always seems

Sometimes it is a sad day
And we almost lost our way
But all we can do now is
That we can only simply pray

All innocence is just gone
And the life is no longer long
May be we don't acknowledge
But we all are doing wrong

Every joy of every day is lost
And life is almost not in cost

Still we can look and see
That all hearts are covered in frost

Many wars are fought
Many more sins are taught
We still do many mistakes
And hope not to be caught

None is ready to take blame
And always pushing towards fame
As advanced as we are
But we are still all untamed

Ah! Too much pride
And we need a guide
We know we'll deny
And behind lies we hide

In rule of hurting others
And in betraying brothers
So many are forgetting
To appreciate the mothers

Soon the lies are fed
Filling all heart 'n' head
Through all of these years
Innocent blood has been shed

So many children are abandoned
All lonely and stranded
Don't know why we all are
Wasting the precious life
That we have been handed

Don't understand why the poor
Are loving no more as humans
Though they are fighting to be free
And ending up the starting war

So many soldiers killed
And there absence can't be filled
So pay close attention
For pure souls have been tilled

We all need to find peace
Work together like breathe
But greatest of all is That
The hate needs to cease

□

40

FLOWERS

Flower
A simple flower
I shall take
For another soul
To smile and awake

Seldom it is used
For love and passion
Or may be some times
For sympathy and compassion

Tulips, roses, blossom and lily
All are so nice and
Have peaceful clarity
Flowers do know and understand
What are our intentions
And they do serve
Without any hesitation

Flowers
They are like mother's expression

Which are priceless 'n' full of emotions
And it is like lover's impression
With lots of honest obsession

Very hard some days when we search for words
Then we get only one alternative to hold
Just to share it with Flowers behold
Like we recite thousand sweet poems
Or sing melodious songs to cherish 'n' pamper
But we can say it all with bunch of Flowers
And say that yes we care

Flowers say our emotional soulful feeling
And it always works to the blissful thinking
We should be thankful to little sweet fragrance of flower
Just like Language without poems is incomplete
It seems like our life as a Garden without flowers is not also complete

□

41

THE MAZE

Life
It is like a maze
No one knows where
It ends up
But that is the only way
Life is played

There comes many turns in life
But we should rise but sometimes
Anyone can fall too but don't feel crime
Just be determined for one thing
That one day you'll stand even more tall

Life
It is like a maze
Where at one way
We are free
And on the other
We have to pay

When one way is right
And one way is wrong
There is only now
Or it is gone

But be sure to yourself
That you'll rise over the wall
And that for sure someday
You'll rise above them all

Like the Almighty sun
Which never dies
Though sets everyday
But only again to rise

Like the terrific ocean
Who has many tides
Sometimes they are down
But invariably they rise

Like the splendid trees
Though they rise from seeds
And go to the heights so great
That they rise 'n' rise 'n' rise

Life
It is like a maze
You will see it
You will feel it
And someday it turns to a challenge
And you meant to be prove it

So after falling once
Or twice or thrice
Fall again 'n' again
But be sure to rise and rise high
After every fall
Just rise a little long

□

42

SHADOW

He wasn't just someone in my life,
but a part of me!
He was someone
whom I look forward to cuddle
at every happy or sad time of my day.

He was someone who never judged me,
Rather he always loved me despite everything.
He was not a person, but
Its like shadow without which
People don't have a life.

And today he left me
And, I am unable to figure out any way
To bring him back.
I wish wherever he is now
He is happier than ever.

My shadow might have left me
But also taught me what it is to live.
I will miss you! My Shadow!
I will miss all those walks and hugs
And running around.

You were the one I started my day with
And the one whom I ended it with.
No one can ever be what you were to me
And I promise to love you the same forever.
You would always be more
than just a part of me.
You will always be...
my shadow...... forever till I live!

□

43

VISION

In the vision of your sparkling eyes
I want to know what all you see
Because every time I look into them
It's not always that the reflection is of me.

In the widest range of universes
Where so many glistening stars are born
And gas clouds always swirl
Where suns and moons shine

All I can see are the different worlds
Where in every corner and amongst everyone
You are one and only... mine.

Very rarely it's been known
That I've been losing all my life;
Now all I want to get is a joyous win.
And thus I've locked sights on the light.

But I don't know one thing
if I'll survive the dark night

Which is all beside me.
I've been running this race of life
But barely tried to get being survived.

I can sense the bright light
but my whole walkway is cloudy.
So, I've been just wishing,
But then I think
what is the use of wishing.

We know we can make a decision
that definitely can change the world.
For so long I've been praying,
That if I will leave someday
Then don't let me get back home.

I'm lost inside the tunnel
Staring down the barrel
I'm running like a bullet
And you can watch me explode.

I never chose my beginning;
But I'm sure I'll write my name
Big, Bright, Bold and with fame
Accompanying... sincerely yours
Just written... in the ending.

□

44

MY STAR

My star you are... in the distance
You have... all my heart.
Although we are different
And we are... not so apart
My star when you shine
Like a low blue light
That burns hot to hotter
Than my yellow and too bright light.

My star you are... in the distance
You have... all my heart
Although we are different
And we are... not so apart.
Your smile is sweet when smiling
Always asking... give me more
You are having radiance which is engulfing
All the way to... reach to the core.

My star you are... in the distance
You have... all my heart
Although we are different
But we are... so near inside not apart.

My star you are... I wanna wake up to
The star no one can take from me
You are the bright star
that guides me through the dark
The one that lightens up my night
You are that blue star
that shows me what true beauty is.

My star you are
The glittering star that shines brightly
in the night sky.
You are the star that will shine forever
in my eyes.
My star you are
To keep and admire.
I wish upon a star
That... someday
you'll be my real star
And forever will be mine.

□

45

GIRL CHILD

A girl child is a God's gift to anyone
A blessing cherished by some or one
A treasure to oneself and family is a girl
The strength keeping morals high is if we possess a girl
Every nation should be proud that its future lies through a girl
Though we give them little care and less pampering than what she needs
But she's always there quite near to heart
Girl is like a handful of warmth
Girl is like heartful of love
We lift the family if
We educate a girl
So let's make them smile
And give them happiness
As girls are precious
And our priceless asset
Girl eyes are also full of dreams
The rare and dared dreams
Girl can also fly high into space
Girl can also dive deep into ocean

Girl can climb snowy mountain peaks
Girl can also travel the coldest Antarctic
Girl can also stand shoulder to shoulder with anyone
Girl is the woman of today and can live with great plan
Girl can also beat all tyranny or demeaning plan
Girl can also defeat any contrary game plan
Girl child of today is full of potential
Let them metamorphose
Into a beautiful flower with full bloom
Girl is delicate but strong, beautiful and fragrant
Girl is the future of humanity
Don't let a girl stop her growth
Because if you chop her wings
You'll crash your tomorrow
Girl is the primal force
Girl is not a toy
Girl is the womb of creation
Her hand rocks the cradle
Girl is men's real salvation!

Always we should feel proud
For being blessed by a girl child
We are having the future and all the blessings from
Almighty beside!

□

46

EARTH

Earth is going to die
because it's not green...
Lives are going to cry
because it's not clean,
Earth is our natured Mother,
We shouldn't pollute it,
She gives us shelter and food,
We should just salute it...

With global warming around
Earth is in danger
Let's make efforts to save it
by becoming a strong ranger...
trees and animals are vanishing,
Earth is in sorrow,
We should make green today
and surely protect it as green tomorrow...

With all the melting snow,
Sigh... one day it will sink,
Rare possibility to save it,
Don't be selfish, just think...

Trees are so much precious,
We should preserve them,
Water is a priceless treasure,
We should reserve it...

We should grow more trees,
To make Mother Earth green,
We have to reduce pollution
and make our Earth a queen
Once just ask a question to yourself
Can earth be Earth?
When all its trees are gone,
And water becomes unhealthy,

And poisoned life no longer greets the dawn
With terrific scary sounds that
death has caused to quit?
Will trees no longer wave, with limbs so clean?
On this hollow earth, that ever in orbit roams?
Will human ego sacrifice the world
To fulfil & its lust for big rich homes?
Will distant space look down and be gone?

I now can hear the mother say,
"I was once called Earth. But now,
very often, I weep. That treeless
planet is no longer Earth."

Save Trees! Save wildlife!
Save water! Save natural resources!

SAVE MOTHER EARTH!

□

47

MOTHER

Someone asked me about what my Mom does?
I thought to myself, that space to be described is small
too
How to write about what all she do
How to write down what all she covers
She plays the role of a nurse
when I fell and my knee is hurted
She plays the role of a governess
when I didn't clean my room.
She plays the role of a designer
when my clothes are hard to match.
She plays the role of a tailor
when my dress needed a patch.
She plays the role of a teacher
when I asked a question.
She becomes a priest
when I had a confession.
She acted as a psychiatrist
when I came home crying.
She plays as a preacher
when I got caught lying.

She becomes a singer
when she sung me to sleep.
She becomes a lifeguard
when she said the water's too deep.
There are many many more,
yet the best one to me,
She is my best friend, and
mine forever she'll be.
She's the strongest woman
I will ever know.
Now Mom's hands may
seem crippled and meek.
She flinches when you bump
them and her grip is quite weak.
But with these hands
she shows a reflection of the woman inside,
Though burdened with limits,
But still so strong with pride.
When opening a flask
seems too great a task,
it's only after great trials that she finally asks.
Don't let yourself mislead you
for you must understand.
It's not what they can't do,
but rather what they can.
These hands have the strength to raise a family right,
to wipe away every tear and hold you real tight.
They come together each day in prayer,
and whenever you need them,
they're always right there.
So, if these hands don't appear all that tough,
Remember they're full of tenderness and love and for
me,

that's enough for a life-time to cherish
A mother is a mother always
Whatever generation it is
Whether it's in retro phase or in reality you see.

□

48

EDUCATION

It is the light of our life
A perfect gift of academic rife

It is the key to a bright and rewarding future
A non-sticky glue that joins our dreams like a suture

It is a path to divine success
A buttery smooth drive to our greatness

It gives our thinking a different appearance
And helps us to drive away all our ignorance

It leads us to the path of prosperity
And gives us our tomorrow with a sounding security

It is the process of teaching and learning
Which will always nurture us in our future earning

It is shaping our true character: is the motto
Leading us to a successful life: the major factor

It is the progressive discovery of our true self
And somewhat the exploitation of the potentials of oneself
It is a better safeguard of liberty than a standing army
A life-saving boat that sees us through our days of storm

It is a ray of academic brilliance
And the backbone of inner resilience
It is the key to unlock the golden door of freedom
And brilliant stage of our rise to stardom

It is a life-sustaining material
Without it, we can't lead a life which is congenial

It is not all about bookish knowledge
But it is also about thorough practical knowledge

It makes a person stand up on his own toes
And strengthen a person to fight with all his foes

It is a fundamental foundation
Whatever the country, state or nation

It is a thick line between right and wrong
A stepping ladder that takes us to the height where we belong

It is Mother of all professions
That help us to acquire all our possession

Education is our birth right
For in it, our future is glistening and bright.

□

49
NATURE

Nature is so beautiful
Nature is so much fun
Either we love it or hate it
But nature is something to love
The nature is god's gift to us
Ahhhh! The Nature

Nature we always love
We cultivate and feed nature
Nature gives us water and feeds us
God gave us nature
We can't live without it
As nature makes us.

I know nature
Nature is so beautiful
Nature is about the earth
Nature has flowers and weeds
What is in nature is us

Our NATURE...

When the beautiful morning arrives
The rays of rising sun welcome her
When the garden of nature open its heart
The garden of flowers hugs her to be near.
When the trees dance to the tune of wind
The birds singing to the nature's choir in rhyme

When the gentleness of nature is filled with pleasure
Then the earth gets showered with the raining weather
When the nature forgets its vastness
Then the God shows her how big her places on earth
Let us thank God for his creation to nurture
And the eyes to see this lovely gift called Nature!!

□

50
HUMANITY

Humans.
We must remember that
it is the human
that makes up humanity.
I am a testament to humanity,
Though we all are ...together,
But all of us different ...yet human,

Stares are blank and sheets of gray
And destructive heartaches here to stay
Vibrant colors becoming bland
Thick and rich mud turning to sand
Nowadays.....
Bodies are lifeless and icy cold
hearts are young but minds are
old empty humans and empty
street strength and insanity comes
to meet Stares are blank and sheets
of grey empty humans here to stay.

BUT THIS IS ALSO TRUE
that

A single Human,
Is alone and weak,
Unable to comprehend the insignificance of its life.
But as a whole... Humanity,
we are unmeasurable, overwhelming
We are filling space and time
with our vivid existence.
We consume all other entities
with our devastating force.
Embodied in thousands
upon thousands of infinitesimal beings.

Being Human...
we can get better humanity

□□□